MW01608246

JOE BIDEN

Table of Contents

Introduction

Joseph Robinette Biden, Jr. has spent most of his adult life in politics. Born in the fall of 1942, the former vice president grew up and experienced his early adulthood during a particularly intriguing period of American history. The first 13 years of his life were spent in Scranton, Pennsylvania. His early life was marked with several difficulties, including a stutter that made him self-conscious and a family move to Mayfield, Delaware, in 1955.

Growing up in a politically restless period in American history changed not only his focus on football and parties but also his career trajectory. Influenced by his early difficulties and by the speeches of President John F. Kennedy, Biden's role in the Democratic Party began to take an increasingly greater role in his life. By 1970, he had begun to transition from practicing law to pursuing a political career.

Between college and the early 1970s, Biden married and had three children. Family tragedy soon derailed his political aspirations in 1972.

when his wife and one-year-old daughter were killed in an auto accident. Difficulty and tragedy have peppered Biden's life, while his perseverance and general affability have often garnered personal and political support from those who know him.

Biden's political ambitions have often encountered obstacles that changed his role within the Democratic Party. Sometimes he won his bids for various political offices; other times, he failed. Biden rose to national prominence when Democratic presidential candidate Barack Obama selected him to be his vice-presidential running mate. Biden was often an interesting foil to Obama's more serious and measured persona. In comparison, Biden was folksy and more off-the-cuff. This helped him become the front runner among the many Democratic presidential candidates when he announced in 2019 that he was running for President.

Biden is a colorful political personality who has had a continually evolving outlook resulting from his having witnessed the Civil Rights movement and from his many ups and downs, both in his personal and professional life. Only time will tell if his willingness to compromise and evolve will prove to be a political liability or a political asset.

Chapter 1

Early Life

Born November 20, 1942, Joseph Robinette Biden, Jr. came from humble beginnings during a troubled period in American history. The US had entered World War II less than a year before he was born, so Biden's early childhood in Scranton, Pennsylvania, was somewhat unsettled because of world events.

His father worked as both a furnace cleaner and a used-car salesman. Biden has often credited both of his parents as essential figures in his life, particularly during the early years. According to him, they were the people who instilled a sense of both toughness and hard work in him. Over time, these traits seem to have translated into resilience and tenacity, which helped him persevere through some profoundly dark periods of his life.

When he was ten years old, his family moved to Delaware, the state that he has considered home ever since. His father sought improved opportunities to better support his six-person family. The Bidens finally settled in Mayfield, Delaware when Biden was 13 years old. They lived in a middle-class neighborhood located near the DuPont chemical company. He attended Catholic schools for a few years, though it was the illustrious Archmere Academy that he wanted to attend for high school.

When his dream of being accepted into Archmere Academy was finally realized, he knew that his family could not afford the full tuition for the prestigious school, so the teenager took on work cleaning the school's windows and weeding the grounds to supplement what his parents could afford to pay toward tuition. Attending the school had long been his dream, and he learned to work hard for the things that he wanted.

His time at the prestigious school proved to be a good experience as he met the challenges of his schoolwork while playing football and working. His grades show that Biden was a solid student, though not exceptional. Despite being a skinny teenager, he enjoyed playing football, with his coach later reportedly saying that Biden was among his best pass receivers.

During his time at the school, Biden made his first foray into being a representative as he ran for student body president. He was elected, but the school blocked him from accepting the position because he had received too many demerits to represent the students.

Biden graduated in 1961 as the US was entering another very tumultuous period. While his grades were not stellar, he managed to graduate with acceptable grades while working and playing sports. It showed that he was able to establish a balance between the different aspects of his life, an ability that he would need later in his life.

Chapter 2

Early Adversities

Biden has quoted his father as saying, "Champ, the measure of a man is not how often he is knocked down, but how quickly he gets up." This has been something that Biden has proven that he has taken to heart through several tragic losses. His mother appears to have instilled a similar fighting spirit, having reportedly responded to his sullenness after being bullied by telling him to "Bloody their nose so you can walk down the street the next day!"

Biden was bullied as a child, in part because of a stutter he had. He was called several nicknames because of the impairment, including "Dash" and "Joe Impedimenta." "Dash" was particularly cruel as it correlated his speech with Morse Code. Another nickname they gave him was "Bye-bye" because he would stutter as he tried to pronounce his last name. Over time, Biden learned to plan what he would say before opening his mouth to better work around his stutter. However, that was not a permanent solution as it was impossible to plan for all scenarios and would certainly have limited his ability to talk to others. Realizing that merely planning his conversations was not adequate, Biden directly took on his stutter (not just his bullies), spending hours reciting poetry at his reflection to work through his impediment.

His family also moved several times, looking for better opportunities. Given Biden's stutter, it was likely difficult as he did not have the same childhood support friendships. His family was not wealthy, and he shared a bedroom with his two brothers and their uncle. Their uncle Edward Blewitt Finnegan was given the nickname "Boo-Boo" so that Biden could more easily pronounce it with his stutter.

In addition to his stutter, Biden had asthma, which later played a role in the direction that his life took.

Chapter 3

College Life

Having graduated with acceptable grades from a prestigious school, Biden was accepted at the University of Delaware, where he decided on a double major: political science and history. This helped to inform him of the unique and often violent history of the US during a time of growing civil unrest in the country.

Despite what appeared to be lofty academic dreams in college, by his own admission, Biden was much more interested in the extra circular aspects of college than the education. During his time in college, it is said that Biden earned probation from a prank that he pulled. According to reports, he used a fire extinguisher to spray the director of one of the University of Delaware dorms.

He has said that his freshman and sophomore years were spent focused more on football and parties than in classes. He also seems to have been rather distracted by women as well. Perhaps this exposure helped to form the person he would become, as the frequent socializing would have made him more aware of the world around him - something that would have been much more difficult if he had kept his nose in his books.

His college career began in 1961 and ended when he graduated in 1964. One of the most important personal events during this time of his life occurred when he went to the Bahamas for spring break during his junior year. On the trip, he met another college student named Neilia Hunter, and he has reportedly said that it was love at first sight for him. Unfortunately, she was a student at Syracuse University in New York. Because of her influence, he began to take a much more serious approach to school, changing the direction his life would take.

Chapter 4

The Changing Times

Biden graduated from high school and college during the 1960s, a time of enormous civil unrest and change. One of the greatest movements of the 20th century was the Civil Rights Movement, and it had a profound impact on the trajectory of Biden's life as figures like Martin Luther King Jr inspired him. Dr. King's speeches called for peaceful resistance to press for equal rights for African Americans. The images of the abuse of the peaceful protesters by law enforcement forced many people to question which side of the law they were on since some of the law enforcement officials were clearly violating the rights of an entire race of people. Anyone who believed that everyone was being treated equally - or who was unaware of the inequality in many American cities and states - was forced to face reality and was often forced to take a side.

Another factor that inspired Biden to pursue politics came from the Kennedy brothers, John and Robert. Biden has specifically cited them as a reason for his interest in becoming a politician. Prior to John F. Kennedy's inauguration, the election of a Catholic to the presidency was often considered to be impossible, as many Americans believed that Catholics were somehow bound by an allegiance to the Pope. Despite being a Catholic, JFK promised that he would make decisions that were right for the country and that Papal decrees would not sway him. As a Catholic, Biden saw the election of the first Catholic President of the US as a sign of the changing times. Becoming president was suddenly a real possibility as JFK proved that religion was not necessarily an impediment to gaining the most powerful position in the nation.

Another major movement occurring at the time was the Anti-Vietnam War Movement that saw the rise of events like Woodstock and the Free Love Movement as people protested against being drafted into the war. Considering the fact that they did not have the right to vote for the politicians who were sending them off to war, teenagers saw this as an injustice. As a result of their activities, the Twenty-Sixth Amendment, which changed the legal voting age from 21 to 18, was added to the US Constitution. Biden himself was not accepted into the military because of his asthma. Instead of joining the protests against the war, he chose to go into politics. He did not want to just protest the war. He wanted to end it by becoming a politician who could actually affect the change that he believed people wanted.

Chapter 5

Marriage and Children

Between the fun of college and the changing times, Biden found his own sense of peace with Neilia Hunter. They met in 1964 and married just two years later. For their wedding, Biden's father gave the newlyweds a 1967 Corvette Stingray, a car that Biden still has today.

Prior to their marriage, Hunter was able to persuade Biden to work harder in college. Finally, taking his education more seriously, Biden was able to gain admittance to the Syracuse University Law School. During this time, he also bought her a puppy, who was then given a name that was a foreshadowing for what was to come within the next decade. The dog's name was Senator.

When he graduated from the University of Delaware in 1965, he moved to live nearer to the woman he loved while he sought to become a lawyer. While he was not a particularly exceptional student, Biden did perform well. However, it was during his time in the law school that he failed a class because of what appeared to be plagiarism when he did not properly cite one of his sources in a paper he wrote. This came back to haunt him later when Biden moved into politics. Nonetheless, he did earn his law degree and passed the bar exam.

In 1966, Biden and Hunter married, and they moved to his home state of Delaware. The most logical place for a new lawyer was Delaware's biggest city, Wilmington, where he quickly got a position at a law firm. He simultaneously worked as a public defender in the city.

It did not take long before he and his wife had their first child, Joseph (Beau) Biden III, who was born in 1969, followed one year later by Hunter Biden, followed one year later by Naomi Biden.

Chapter 6

Joining the Democratic Party

Soon after moving to Wilmington, Delaware, Biden finally joined one of the two major American political parties. Since joining the Democratic Party, Biden has remained an active member, meaning he has been a Democrat for more than four decades.

While he was still in his 20s, Biden was fairly easily swayed to do things that the party wanted him to do, such as run for elected office. This began to shift his interest away from the legal profession and back toward his early experiences of running for elected positions. However, the transition was not immediate. During 1971, while an elected official on the New Castle County Council, he began a new law firm.

The needs of his growing family, the shifting needs of his political party, and the fallout from the 1960s all influenced Biden to change what he could from the different positions for which he ran as a member of the Democratic Party. Though he had not been a member of the party for very long, he quickly gained attention within the Democratic Party, who soon asked him to run for the Senate in 1972. This was despite his short political career at that point. The Democratic Party was facing a particularly difficult run that year, so it was likely that they felt that the charm of the young family man would be a suitable foil to a popular Republican incumbent. The party periodically bet on Biden, and it was the first time that they had encouraged him to seek a substantial role in office.

This run to become a senator was a life-changing event that not only set Biden on the path that eventually saw him as a stalwart member of the Democratic Party, but as a person on whom the party would rely on over the next 40 years.

Despite his checkered successes (he has lost about as often as he has won when running for different political positions), Biden has often been viewed as a stellar member of his party. He learned how to work with Republicans based on the ideals of politics from back in the 1970s when politicians were less inclined to vilify the other party. However, as a member of the Democratic Party, his views have followed the party lines. For the most part, his long history in the party has earned him a reputation as a middle-of-the-road person who can be relied upon to gauge the way the party is going.

Chapter 7

An Uncertain Early Career Path

Like his father, Biden shifted careers several times, though he was much quicker to make changes than his father.

While his family life seemed to be moving quickly and relatively smoothly, his professional life was a mix of successes and failures. Before joining the Democratic party, he worked for a law firm, and he had a part-time role as a public defender. He took on an interesting case as the defender of a fisherman who had stolen a Holstein cow.

He first foray into an elected profession began soon after he arrived in Wilmington when he ran for a position on the New Castle County Council. Just like his run for student body president in high school, he won, this time by 2,000 votes. In this role, he generally worked to stop bigger companies from making changes that would hurt the general public. The most notable project that he fought was a proposed 10-lane highway that would have displaced people in a large number of neighborhoods. Another fight in which he engaged was in preventing the building of refineries along the Delaware coast.

He received calls during his first year on the Council from people in the area who were angered by his support for building public housing. When he received one such call, the caller asked him if he wanted people of color (though the person did not say it in a politically correct way) to live next to him, he responded, "If you're the alternative, I guess the answer is yes."

His success over the first couple of years in this position finally directed him away from law and increasingly toward politics. This helped him to decide to follow the recommendations of the Democratic Party as they pressed him to continue to aim higher.

His success on the New Castle County Council came just two years later with his run to replace the popular Republican senator, J. Caleb Boggs. Biden's charm helped him to pull off a surprising upset, which was precisely what the Democrats had hoped for when they encouraged him to run. At just 29 years old, Biden became the fifth-youngest person to be voted in as a member of the US Senate.

Chapter 8

A Life-Changing Tragedy

A life-changing tragedy soon marred Biden's successful run to be a Delaware Senator. He won the seat in November of 1972, but his family did not get a chance to celebrate his swearing-in. With only a week left before Christmas of 1972, his wife was driving their children around as she shopped for the family Christmas tree. A tractor-trailer struck their car, and his wife and daughter died before they could reach the hospital. His daughter Naomi was only a year and a half old. Although they had survived the accident, both of their sons were critically injured. They were rushed to the hospital, where they remained for several weeks.

Instead of celebrating the holidays and his new office, Biden spent the next few weeks at the hospital as much as he could. He has admitted that it was the first time in his life that he could understand why people would consider suicide, and even contemplated it himself. The despair that he felt over the loss of half of his family was nearly too much for him to bear.

However, he assessed his life and ultimately decided that he also had a responsibility to the people who had elected him. At the same time, he could not leave his sons to recover on their own in the hospital without him.

It was this situation in which Biden entered the national political stage in 1973. Biden's dedication to his family has been one of the elements that has made him sympathetic while gaining him respect from both parties. Instead of sacrificing either his family or his career, Biden found ways to support his family while honoring his obligations to his constituents.

Chapter 9

First Major Political Position

New senators were to be sworn into their seats in Washington, DC, but Biden opted to remain behind in Wilmington, where he was sworn in to his seat while remaining in the hospital room with his son Beau. His dedication to seeing his sons heal did not end with the swearing-in ceremony. He commuted daily from Delaware to Washington, DC, so that he could spend every evening with his sons. Nor did he stop the practice after his sons were released from the hospital. For as long as Biden was a member of the Senate, he continued to take the train to work every morning instead of taking up residence in Washington when the Senate was in session. This meant a one-way commute of 75 minutes every day.

Biden used Amtrak to travel to and from the nation's capital, and he has said that he considers the staff on the train as family. Over the years, he has held parties and invited conductors and other staff members to those events, including barbecues.

During this time, his policies often aligned with conservative Democrats, ranging from his opposition to *Roe v. Wade* to court-ordered school busing. Even if people did not agree with his stands, the charm and honesty that he seemed to express were viewed with respect. By the end of his first six-year term as a Senator from Delaware, Biden had remarried, this time to a schoolteacher. He and Jill Jacobs wed in 1977, and they have a daughter, Ashley. When he took office, Biden's tragic personal situation was likely viewed as a part of his strength of character by the time he finished his first term. He had not only followed through with taking his seat in the Senate despite the recent personal tragedy, but he served the people of Delaware in a way that they felt was an accurate representation of their views and values.

Chapter 10

Senate Career

By the end of a particularly challenging first term, Biden proved to be an incredibly popular senator. His second run for the Senate resulted in a resounding victory, a feat that he repeated several more times. His Senate career lasted for 36 years, going from 1973 until 2009.

Although Biden has been popular, some of the policies that he supported in the early days have come back to haunt him. One such policy came from his early days when Biden opposed the practice of busing schoolchildren across town. During the 1970s and 1980s, the nation was still struggling to implement changes that were required by the US Supreme Court in Brown v. Board of Education in 1954. Things like segregated schools were thought to be justified because some politicians claimed that people should be attending the schools that were close to them. Naturally, this did entail a sort of segregation.

To address this problem, the US Supreme Court issued another ruling for Swann v Charlotte-Mecklenburg Board of Education that required that buses take students to schools further away from their homes so that schools would not remain segregated simply because of location. This proved to be unpopular across the country as it meant students had to go further to school, taking up more of their day. This is the side on which Biden stood, saying that it focused too much on quotas and not enough on actually making the schools more equal. This was one of the times when Biden was not on the side of the majority of Democrats, most of whom agreed with busing. This stance was part of what lost Democrats a lot of their support in northern states, particularly in the suburbs. By siding against busing, Biden may have been able to keep his voters on his side.

The Supreme Court reversed the decision in 1974, which exacerbated the problem instead of helping to end school segregation. It remains a problem today since white Americans moved to the suburbs to keep their kids in predominantly white schools. African Americans were not able to move, as they usually did not have the means to move. Because the schools were not forced to desegregate, schools have continued to remain unequal as the suburban schools tend to receive more funding than urban schools.

During his 36 years in office, Biden has held several prominent positions within the Senate. He served as the Judiciary Committee chair for eight years and the Foreign Relations Committee chair for four years. He was appointed to preside over two of the most contentious US Supreme Court confirmation hearings in recent American history. The first nominee over whose confirmation he presided was Robert Bork, who was eventually rejected by the Senate. The second and more well-known confirmation hearing was of Clarence Thomas, who was accused of sexually harassing one of the women in his office, Anita Hill. Biden's performance during this hearing has also come back to haunt him because the way he treated Hill has earned him considerable chastisement. Reviewing the tapes of the hearings shows a willingness on his part to dismiss her words and his condescending attitude toward her instead of hearing her out or taking her accusation as seriously as people today feel it should have been taken. Biden has expressed his own regrets over the way things happened, though he has not publicly apologized to Hill for the way the Senate treated her.

Although Biden is a well-known national figure, he earned his popularity in Delaware. Some of the work that he performed as a member of the New Castle County Council he continued as Senator. He worked to create a more corporate-friendly climate within Delaware to improve the economy of his state. Among some of his most popular moves, he helped to pass legislation against domestic violence and another bill that put more police on the streets to protect citizens. Among his most contentious moves, he was one of the primary crafters of what is now a controversial anti-crime bill that mandated stricter prison sentences for drug dealing or use, and he supported an assault rifle ban that was in effect until the early part of the 21st century.

As a person who witnessed the Anti-Vietnam War protests, Biden has revealed evolving perspectives on war and foreign policy. For example, he voted against the Gulf War of 1990-1991 when the Iraqi leader Saddam Hussein invaded Kuwait, but he voted for the more controversial Iraq War of 2003-2011, putting him in unpopular camps in terms of his war record.

Chapter 11

An Eye on the Presidency

Biden has never seemed to forget how John F. Kennedy's election affected his own potential political future. After serving in the US Senate for two decades, Biden finally made a major political decision that painted the way he was perceived across the US. He decided to run for President of the United States.

His campaign began in June of 1987 after he announced his intentions. Running for the position has always been incredibly arduous. Though Biden's two sons were adults, he still required the support of his second wife, Jill.

When he started campaigning for the first major election of the Democratic primary, Biden gave a speech at the Iowa State Fair. As the media began to analyze his speech, it became apparent that several portions had been lifted from a speech by Neil Kinnock, a UK Labor MP and Margaret Thatcher challenger. This caused the media to review his academic career and zero in on a potential instance of plagiarism in a law school paper he had written. The negative publicity became the defining part of the campaign. Biden could not remove the negativity, and he left the race in September of that year. At the time, he was presiding over the confirmation hearing of Robert Bork. While the end of his first presidential campaign was negative, Biden continued his work as a senator with a much better understanding of what went into running for the most powerful political position in the country.

Chapter 12

The Plagiarism Scandal

Ultimately, Biden's first presidential run ended because of the plagiarism scandal that began because he failed to properly cite his inspiration for his speech when he was speaking at the Iowa State Fair. However, that was only the first problem that started to snowball into a much larger scandal. It could perhaps have been easy to overlook one transgression, as the presidential candidate had appropriately been citing Kinnock's influence before that speech. The problem was that Biden seemed to have done more than just fail to cite the inspiration. Some have claimed that he went beyond plagiarism and claimed different aspects of other people's lives. For example, he said that he was the first person in his family to attend college or that his ancestors had worked in coal mines, two claims that were not true. Those were facts about Kinnock's life, and not Biden's.

Further criticism was heaped on his campaign as people found more than just similarities between his speeches and several passages from the famous political figures Hubert Humphrey and Robert F. Kennedy.

This was the second time when Biden suffered severe repercussions because he failed to cite a source, though this instance went well beyond just plagiarism. It appeared that he had started to exaggerate and lie about his own experiences. It is challenging to understand why he would invent false personal difficulties when he actually has experienced so much personal tragedy and loss and overcome it in such a very public way.

Unfortunately, even this second accusation of plagiarism does not seem to have resulted in a lesson learned for the presidential hopeful. The ending to Biden's first presidential run returned to the spotlight during his 2020 run for President, particularly as he was again accused of lifting other people's work without citing the source. The climate plan that he presented during 2019 was virtually identical to the plan that was released by the Carbon Capture Coalition. Despite being a clear copy of the plan, the group was not cited as being the authors of the plan.

His staff immediately took the blame for it, saying that they had adopted it without Biden knowing that it was lifted from elsewhere. While it is true that no candidate can be aware of all machinations within their campaigns, adopting and presenting a plan is something that people expect a candidate to understand, both in terms of content and sources. Many of the other candidates were active participants in the making of their plans, so it seems difficult to believe that he did not know.

Biden is indisputably prone to gaffes whether or not he has intentionally plagiarized or lied about his experiences. Even he has described himself as a "gaffe machine." Only time will tell whether voters will view the gaffes as an endearing proclivity or a political liability.

Chapter 13

Life and Career After 1988

After ending his presidential bid in 1987, Biden threw his attentions into the serious work of the Senate. The work that he did during the Bork confirmation hearing gained him some attention as he seemed to set up the conservative judge with questions that appeared to make him look relatable. The way the questions were worded was meant to help Bork to open up as a way to get the Supreme Court candidate to more honestly express his conservative opinions. This included some controversial views without the cover of more obscure legal terminology. As a result of the way the candidate responded to the questions, he was voted down by the Senate 42 to 58.

While this worked well for Biden's political career, the stress of the presidential run, coupled with the intensity of the hearings, may have put a strain on his health. In February of 1988, he collapsed and was taken to the hospital where he was diagnosed as having a brain aneurysm. The doctors were able to successfully repair the damage after two major surgeries. As a result, Biden was absent from the Senate for seven months.

It took a couple of decades before Biden made any other life-changing decisions. Despite the negativity around his first presidential bid, Biden was not entirely discouraged from making another run for president. As President George W. Bush's' second term was coming to an end in 2007, Biden again decided to run for president. The favored early candidate was former President Bill Clinton's wife, Hillary Clinton, but as the nation had not yet elected a woman, there were many questions around her ability to win in the general election. Apart from her, there were no other strong candidates in the early days.

Then the Iowa Caucus took place. This time, Biden did not seem to attract much media attention, not even negative attention. Having come in fifth during the caucus, Biden decided to drop out of the race - a race that would eventually be won by a one-term senator from Chicago: Barack Obama.

Chapter 14

Obama's Running Mate

When Biden saw no path forward to the Democratic presidential nomination, having only gained 1% of the vote in the first caucus, Obama saw potential in the charming long-time senator. Soon after winning the Democratic nomination, Obama quickly selected Biden to be his running mate. It was certainly an interesting choice as Biden had gone after Obama's lack of experience as one of the reasons that people should not vote for the young senator.

Their campaign was against Biden's long-time Senate colleague and friend, John McCain, and his running mate, Sarah Palin, though McCain had not yet chosen his running mate. McCain was quick to use Biden's own words against his running mate, Obama. There was also adequate footage of Biden praising McCain as they had been senators together for decades, and they were friends. In fact, Biden and his wife had convinced McCain to speak to an attractive woman when they were out to dinner. The encouragement resulted in a date, and eventually, to John and Cindy McCain's marriage.

Despite this, both parties were pleased with Obama's choice as Republicans and Democrats viewed the long-serving senator as someone they could work with if Obama were elected. The US Senate and the vice president often work together, with the vice president acting as the tiebreaker when there is a 50-50 split in a vote in the Senate. Obama himself said that the reason he chose Biden was because of the senator's extensive political experience, particularly in foreign affairs, of which Obama had little experience. Biden was also seen as Obama's foil, someone who could speak well, if long-winded, and who was willing to challenge Obama's ideas. Obama did not want someone who would simply agree with him, but someone who would present other ideas.

The two parties were each running with a first:e Obama as the first African American elected to represent a party for the presidency, and Palin as the first woman elected to represent the other party for the position of Vice President. While the two presidential candidates had some rather fierce back and forth during the presidential debates, Biden was in a much different position facing the largely unknown Governor of Alaska.

Palin had minimal political experience until that point and turned out to be as gaffe-prone as Biden, perhaps even more so. Her gaffes were mercilessly satirized by late-night hosts and the long-running *Saturday Night Live* television show. Because of Biden's decades of experience, people turned into the vice-presidential debates to see just how Biden would treat not only the first prominent female figure vying for one of the two most prominent positions in the country but someone who had far less political experience.

Ultimately, Biden was restrained, particularly compared to the media. He came across as more sympathetic and not out to make her look bad, something that earned him much respect across the country, particularly given her apparent ignorance on how to respond to some of the questions during the debate. Some saw it as being condescending, but, for the most part, people praised him for taking a more measured and restrained approach. The debates presented him as someone who was able to read the room and to better face the opposition with a sense of respect that was largely eroding during that period of American politics.

Ultimately, many of the potential problems that Biden would face if he were to run for president again came up when he was Obama's running mate. This could have been one of the reasons why he was less eager to jump into the Democratic primary following Obama's second term. From Biden's support of the increasingly unpopular Iraq War of 2003 to the way he treated Anita Hill during Thomas's US Supreme Court confirmation hearing to his opposition to abortion, many people viewed his record negatively. No longer focused as much on the plagiarism scandal, it was his record that was suddenly playing against Biden as the pair ran on the Democratic ticket for 2008.

Chapter 15

Two Terms as the Vice President

Obama and Biden were successful in their bid for office, winning 52.9% of the popular vote - though the election results were based on the electoral college results and not the popular vote. Before being sworn in to his new position, Biden had to resign his position as a senator. This he did on January 15, 2009. Five days later, Obama was sworn in as the 44th President, and Biden as the 47th Vice President of the United States. Obama and Biden went on to win a second term in 2012 when they faced Mitt Romney and Paul Ryan. Biden's performance during the vice-presidential debates was much more aggressive and animated against Paul Ryan than it had been against Sarah Palin.

As the Vice President, Biden was put in charge of more than $785 billion as the nation was going through the Great Recession. As someone who had often kept an eye on the economic conditions in Delaware, then the country as a whole, when he chaired important committees in the Senate, Biden set up a task force to manage the vast sums of stimulus money. Since he had considerable experience with foreign affairs, Biden also took on some serious foreign policy issues. He was instrumental in re-establishing the arms reduction treaty between the US and Russia that had started more than a decade earlier in July of 1991. Called the Strategic Arms Reduction Treaty (START), the US and USSR agreed to reduce the number of nuclear weapons that they had. As the USSR had been dissolved just a few months later (after the original signing), the US had been working with several independent nations since 1992. The treaty had expired at the end of 2009. Biden's work was to reengage with negotiations on START with Russia. The treaty was restarted, and enforcement began on February 5, 2011. Russia and the US had until 2018 to limit its strategic arms.

Biden also gave a speech to the military personnel in Iraq who ended the Iraq War in September 2010. He continued to play a role in the Middle East, criticizing some US allies in the Middle East for strengthening the terrorist group

ISIS while trying to remove the Syrian dictator Bashar al-Assad.

His national work was influenced by his long history in the Senate. Biden was able to work well between the two parties to distribute funds to help the flagging economy while raising taxes quickly. He was instrumental in helping to avoid the financial crisis that the nation faced, working closely with the Republican Senator Mitch McConnell. While the Senate Republicans made a very public display of opposing Obama, they were more than willing to work with their long-time colleague for the good of the country.

As the number of public shootings was on the rise, Biden entered the national debate on gun control. One of the primary catalysts was the Newtown, Connecticut, school shooting, after which the nation seemed ready to pass some kind of gun control legislation. Though Congress was unmoved to act, Biden presented Obama with 19 different actions that the President could take without Congressional approval to start to curb gun violence.

While there were some apparent differences in their way of thinking, images of Obama and Biden together suggested a solid friendship between the pair. They openly ribbed each other and joked around, something that had become relatively uncommon between the men in the two positions over the previous decades. This relationship played a role in how people perceived Biden during his 2020 run for the presidency.

Tragedy again struck Biden's family in 2015 when his eldest son, Beau, died at the age of 46. He succumbed to brain cancer, a disease that took Biden's long-time friend, John McCain, just a few years later. Biden seemed to pull away from the spotlight to mourn the loss of his son.

With his son's death still so recent, Biden did not appear to require much time to consider whether he should run for the presidency again. He cited the loss of his son as one of the reasons he was not going to run for the Democratic ticket. This is not a usual move in American politics, especially as he was the Vice President during the presidency of Barack Obama - a popular political figure. Although Obama was somewhat divisive in some circles, he was still popular when he left office in 2017. Biden might have stood a better chance of defeating the Republican candidate than Hillary Clinton (the Democratic candidate) as she had long been a more divisive figure in

American politics. She and the Republican candidate went on to be the two least popular presidential candidates in modern American history. Given Biden's recent loss, though, it is easy to understand why he was unwilling to engage with the kind of questioning and publicity that is the increasingly sensational and hostile media approach to dealing with candidates for public office. When he addressed the question of whether or not he would run for president, Biden responded that the door had closed on the possibility of him running for the position.

Before leaving office, President Obama awarded Biden the Presidential Medal of Freedom, which is the highest honor that an American citizen can earn. Obama was effusive in his praise of Biden's work and abilities. Biden responded with an unplanned speech in which he thanked Obama, the first lady, and his own family for all of their support. Unlike other presidents and vice presidents, the two seem to have formed a very close bond on full display as they finally left their respective roles after eight years of side-by-side work.

Chapter 16

Life After the Vice Presidency

Having closed the door on running for the presidency following the end of Obama's second term, Biden entered a new stage of his life. He no longer held a public position. Despite not holding a political position, Biden was not silent about the direction the country was taking under President Trump. He was a vocal opponent to many of the changes and actions taken by the new government, earning him some criticism by Republicans and conservative media outlets who thought that he should not openly disparage the administration after his term in office. However, Democrats have been quick to point out how openly hostile Donald Trump and conservative media outlets were during the eight years of Obama and Biden's time in office.

Trump had been a loud proponent of a right-wing conspiracy theory that Obama was not an American citizen, yet he never provided any evidence to support the claim. Having found an audience willing to believe him in the conservative media, Trump continued to spread the unfounded theory until Obama finally produced a copy of his American birth certificate. While it did not entirely stop the conspiracy theory, it did severely hamper the unfounded claims that Obama was not born in the United States. Biden did not appear to forgive or ignore the problems that Trump had caused the Obama Administration through several years of pushing the conspiracy theory. Now that Trump was in public office himself, Biden had no problem speaking out against what he saw as some of the biggest breaches in decorum, apparent illegal activities of the Trump administration, and general failings of the 45th president.

After the first year of the Trump Administration, Biden's statement that the window for him to run for president was not closed for 2020. He began by ruminating that, if he had run for President in 2016, he would likely have won. This belief seems to have influenced his decision on the 2020 presidential race. When speaking with Oprah Winfrey during an interview in November 2017, he said that a person needed to answer two questions before declaring his intentions.

The person needs to decide if they are the most qualified person to take on the burden of becoming the leader of the US. This is based not only on their qualifications but also on the current condition of the nation when they are running. For example, one of the reasons that Abraham Lincoln is considered one of the best presidents in the nation's history was because of the situation in which he assumed the role. He seemed to be the right person for that particular period, but may not have been had he been elected at a different period in American history. Biden admitted that he felt that he was the best qualified at that point in time, so it was the answer to the second question that had prevented him from running.

If the person thinks they are the best qualified at that particular point, will they be able to dedicate themselves fully? With his son having recently died, Biden knew that he would not be able to dedicate himself to doing what was required fully. He was still mourning the loss of a child and was in no emotional state to properly handle the problems that are part of running for President.

Just a few weeks after he spoke with Winfrey, he was on another television program, *The View*.

This time he was interacting with a panel of women, including the daughter of his long-time colleague and friend John McCain. McCain had recently been diagnosed with the same brain cancer that had killed Beau, and Meghan McCain was one of the hosts of *The View*. The panel had begun talking to Biden about his son, and Meghan McCain became upset as her father was just beginning the same difficult fight. When the two parties were obstructing each other and refusing to work together, the touching scene of the Democrat Biden taking the Republican McCain's hand and giving her words of consolation and hope struck a chord with the people. It showed that there was still some sympathy and ability to look beyond politics to see the humanity in the other side.

All of the publicity that Biden had been receiving since he had begun to speak out against Trump led to the media asking him about his thoughts on running for president in 2020. Considering the political cycle had only recently ended, it was a rather premature question, but Biden had already been thinking about it. When asked about the odds he would run in the spring of 2018, Biden responded that he had not yet ruled out the possibility. This is often taken as a sign that a run is inevitable. He expressed the hope that someone else would be able to take on the mantle because he felt that some great candidates could also run. Ultimately though, he felt that the Democrats needed to put someone forward who could beat the current president.

Chapter 17

A New Presidential Bid

Almost since the inauguration of President Trump, people had been asking Biden if he would run in 2020. Despite his not giving a definitive answer, polls included him in trying to determine who stood the best chance of winning a place on the Democratic ticket. In June 2018, a poll was conducted by Harvard CAPS/Harris, and it showed that Democrats were not ready to give up on the possibility of Biden running for president. According to that poll, Biden was the leading Democrat to win the ticket, gaining 32% of the vote from those who participated. However, the poll (like most polls) should be taken with a grain of salt as the second leading figure was Hillary Clinton, who had lost to Trump just a couple years earlier. It showed an inability within the party to let go of their most prominent people, even if those people had already proven they did not perform as well as the party had hoped.

Biden's potential run was tarnished even before he announced his candidacy. During his time as Vice President, Biden had gained a reputation for being a little over-enthusiastic about invading women's personal space. This became a problem when Lucy Flores submitted an essay to a publisher accusing Biden of inappropriately kissing her when he had been out on a campaign event. Biden largely dismissed this as being a part of who he was, and that he had spent decades hugging, kissing, and displaying affection. He followed up the dismissal by saying that he had never intended for the affection to be anything more than a friendly gesture. Biden noticeably failed to apologize for what she claimed was inappropriate behavior but said he would listen if anyone had a complaint or believed that he had acted inappropriately. Flores' accusation was followed by several more accusations from women who were uncomfortable with his overfamiliarity and willingness to touch them.

The issue was largely forgotten when, in April 2019, Biden finally announced that he was running. It was not a surprise but an expectation. Many other potential Democrats had jumped into the contest for the presidential nomination, and they had been working toward becoming the frontrunner for a couple of months by the time Biden joined the candidates.

As a part of his announcement video, Biden pointed to the tragedy in Charlottesville, Virginia, which saw the murder of a protester against a right-wing rally when a white supremacist drove a car into the protesting crowd. According to Biden, the nation was facing a threat that they had not seen in his lifetime, particularly as the rally included Neo-Nazis.

Many people expected Barack Obama to endorse his friend from the beginning of Biden's run for office. However, it was only after he became the presumptive Democratic candidate that Obama finally spoke out to endorse him for the position.

Biden faced a difficult struggle, both because of his record and because some viewed him as a part of an entrenched political system. As the Republicans moved increasingly further toward conservatism, Senator Bernie Sanders had helped to significantly push the Democratic party to a more progressive agenda because of his platform while running for the Democratic ticket in 2016. There were increasingly fewer people in the center, which was where Biden had spent much of his political career. He needed to resonate with the increasingly progressive direction of the party, but Biden was unable to tap into the youthful vote that was drawn to participate as a part of Sanders' campaign.

Easily the biggest strike against Biden was his record, particularly relating to women and his early stance on abortion. During the Democratic debates, his position in the 1970s of opposing federal mandates for busing drew further criticism when Democratic hopeful Kamala Harris pointed out that his opposition would have adversely affected her. She said that she was a child who had benefited from the mandate for the short period that it had been enacted.

Following the criticism on his national record, Biden began to lean into his record of working with foreign nations. At the time, relationships with many long-time allies were tense, and he highlighted how he already had an established relationship with them that could help improve America's international relationships.

A more sinister accusation was made during September 2019 when Trump was recorded asking the president of the Ukrainian government to start an investigation into how

Hunter Biden, Joe's son, had gained his position with one of the Ukrainian energy companies. Trump's request led to his impeachment in the Democrat-controlled House of Representatives. According to the impeachment charges, Trump abused his power to undermine a political rival. The impeachment trial was rushed, and Trump was acquitted in the Republican-controlled Senate in early 2020.

During this time, Biden appeared to be floundering in the polls. He failed to gain any substantial votes until the South Carolina primary, where he outperformed all of the other Democrats. Despite having performed better in other states, many of the Democratic hopefuls dropped out following their loss in South Carolina. This is perhaps ironic because the Democrats allowed their candidate to be chosen based on primary results from a state that always votes for Republicans. Despite having no chance of winning South Carolina in the general election, the Democrats took his victory as a sign that Biden was the most electable middle-of-the-road Democrat to run for the office of President. This was despite his poor performance and numerous gaffs on the campaign trail.

By March 2020, Biden and Sanders were the only remaining Democrats running for the position. Their efforts to campaign were significantly curtailed and complicated as Covid-19 began to spread across the nation. The two candidates agreed that holding rallies and debates with audiences was too risky. They had a debate without an audience, during which Biden committed himself to have a woman as his running mate should he become the Democratic nominee. With more states holding their primary elections, Sanders soon realized that he would not be able to overcome the lead that Biden had amassed, and he bowed out of the race.

Soon after becoming the presumed Democratic nominee, Biden was hit with another allegation as Tara Reade accused him of sexual assault. Though he had been accused of a serious crime by one of his former aides, Biden remained the presumptive nominee. Strangely, Reade came out to say that she still supported him for president over Trump, who had more than a dozen accusations of sexual assault before his own election in 2016.

If Biden is elected, he will be the oldest person to be elected to the position. This has inspired some to call for an upper age limit for the office, just as there is a minimum, 35-year, age limit.

Chapter 18

Evolving Perspectives

Some politicians are praised for holding to their position. Other politicians are praised for being able to admit when they are wrong and to let that guide them to do better. These politicians are also said to waffle between decisions or are accused of pandering to their constituents simply to stay in office.

During the 1970s, Biden went on the record as being firmly against Roe v Wade, which made abortions legal. Another divisive stance Biden has held pertains to gun ownership. He has become active in trying to curb gun violence across the nation, and he has plans to implement stricter gun control that is meant to keep the weapons out of the hands of people who are at greater risk of using them to commit crimes.

Less divisive today is his stance on gay marriage. When gay marriage was being actively debated prior to the *Obergefell v. Hodges* Supreme Court ruling in 2015, Biden came out in favor of it. It has been reported that this initially upset then-President Obama as he had not openly supported what today is largely considered a part of equal rights for all Americans. This shows how he and the president were not always on the same page, and how it did sometimes adversely affect their relationship, though Obama did come out in favor of gay marriage not too much later. At the time, they were just beginning their bid for a second term, which was why Obama was upset. As one prominent Democrat had come out in favor of it, this pushed the issue even further to the forefront of American politics.

Conclusion

Joseph Biden has had an extensive political history, and it has often been affected by personal tragedy and his political relationships. During a time when Democrats and Republicans have been entirely hostile towards one another, he maintained a healthy working relationship with another long-time senator, John McCain. His willingness to work with others that he did not necessarily agree with has earned him a considerable amount of criticism during a time when both parties seem incapable of accomplishing important things because they refuse to work together.

With his humble beginnings as the eldest son of a blue-collar worker and several personal tragedies, Biden has demonstrated an ability to overcome several very difficult circumstances. When many politicians were using their positions to enrich themselves, Biden appeared on a list of least wealthy political officials in 2014, coming in at rank 577 out of 581 officials. Only time will tell whether Joe Biden's history, record, personality, strengths, weaknesses, and quirks will doom or propel his second run for President of the United States.

Manufactured by Amazon.ca
Bolton, ON